CASH AFTER A CRASH

"An accident attorney's perspective on settling
with insurance companies and getting
the most money for your claim"

Dear Reader,

You made a smart decision in choosing to read this book.

Every year, thousands of people like you are in automobile crashes. You'd be surprised to discover how many of your neighbors and people in your region have gone through exactly what you are dealing with now.

I want you to know that there's a path for you. By reading this book, you've taken the first step to getting the best possible settlement. You could have ignored this and kept on sifting through random pieces of information on the internet. Instead, you now have a comprehensive resource for settling your claim.

Let me tell you about a former client of mine. Michelle was 36 years old when she was involved in a bad car accident. She was transported by a rescue team to the local hospital, where she was diagnosed with a broken ankle. Michelle contacted my office immediately, and we started gathering and investigating all information relevant to her accident. Michelle later underwent surgery for her ankle. She had to have three plates and seven screws inserted to reset her ankle. Michelle's surgeon did an excellent job, but Michelle has to live with this injury for the rest of her life. With our help, and following the strategies outlined in this book, we were able to settle Michelle's claim for a seven figure sum. While Michelle would definitely rather not have gone through this ordeal, her life has been changed forever. It's extremely important that you note that not all cases get the same results.

This story is one of many that we have handled at The DeVries Law Firm, P.A.

Once you've looked through this information, feel free to call us to discuss your legal issue. If it were up to me, I would insist that we have a conversation, just because I know how much it helps to speak with someone about these matters. Hopefully you'll take me up on this offer to talk. Until then, I hope this information provides you with guidance and clarity.

Sincerely,
Shawn A. DeVries, J.D., M.B.A.

P.S. We're just a phone call away at 904.348.0030. Make sure to mention that you've read our book. We're ready to answer whatever questions you may have.

TABLE OF CONTENTS

Preface

For a long time, many drivers and passengers who have been involved in road traffic accidents have lost or limited their claims due to a lack of knowledge about how the insurance industry operates. While there are many documents and articles written about insurance covers, there is no comprehensive guide to policyholders on how to get the best settlement after an accident.

The auto insurance industry tends to thrive on "secrets." This book unveils the secrets of the auto insurance sector, and how you can best use these to your advantage. This is the guide you have been waiting for. It begins with the fascinating history of insurance, dating back centuries ago. It's a good way to start our discussion.

Chapter One introduces you to present-day insurance. It touches on the laws of insurance in different states, with an emphasis on Florida's laws. As you read on, take note of how the book emphasizes the importance of involving a lawyer in every step you take.

Chapter Two goes on to define the auto insurance policies and how they come in to play after an accident. Chapter Three instructs policyholders on how to conduct themselves at the scene of the accident. It tells you, the policyholder, what to do and what not to do immediately after the accident

Chapters Four through to Ten elaborately explain topics including: factors affecting your insurance claims, how to get your medical bills paid after an accident, fraud in the insurance industry and subrogation (third party carriers). Chapter Seven offers you rare information about accidents involving Uber or Lift vehicles, and offers advice on what to do if you are a casualty of an Uber car accident. It is our sincere hope that this book gives you the much needed guidance you deserve.

CHAPTER I

The History of Insurance

What comes to mind when you hear the word insurance? Perhaps a road accident, fire, terminal illness, property loss or even death? That's understandable, because insurance models were designed as a calculated loss-preparedness scheme. They are crafted to compensate you in the event of a particular occurrence that may result in predefined loss.

Insurance is as old as any other trade. It dates back to around 4000-3000 B.C.E. and was common among Babylonian merchants. It later spread to Hindu and Greek traders in 600 B.C.E. and 4th-century B.C.E. respectively.

Insurance started out as agreements called bottomry contracts. In these arrangements, merchants were granted loans with interest. The interest acted as insurance in case of loss at sea during shipment. If this were to happen, the merchants would not repay the loan: the interest would cover that.

Bottomry was recognised in Ancient Roman law where an agreement was drawn, and funds were left in the custody of a money changer. Marine insurance emerges out of this context, which, having developed gradually over the years, now shapes present-day insurance.

In those days, there were also burial societies in Rome which paid for burial expenses of members from their monthly contributions.

History of Insurance in the United States

Benjamin Franklin is credited to have organized the first American insurance company in 1752. Later, in 1759, the Presbyterian Minister's Fund created the first life insurance company in the American colonies. Many other insurances emerged, and by 1820, New York alone had 17 stock life insurance companies.

The number of life insurance companies grew rapidly over the years, but many failed due to poor management and other systemic issues. Initially, there were few, or sometimes *no* effective regulatory systems put in place, and this placed the companies in a lot of management and financial crises.

Prior to the 1871 Great Chicago Fire and the Francisco earthquake of 1906, there were an estimated 33 insurance companies, and these disasters led to the collapse of many of them.

Another major contributor to the collapse of insurance companies happened in the U.S. Civil War era, during which several malpractices (such as wrong allocation of dividends, exaggerated claims and lack of knowledge to balance the assets and liabilities) saw many other insurance companies go under.

In the 20th century, from 1910 to 1990, life insurance in the United States had realized a steady growth of 8.4%. To date, the United States has a remarkable number of insurance companies offering a wide range of policies.

CHAPTER II

What Type of Insurance Is Best For Me?

Getting the best settlement after an accident requires first of all that you understand the different types of auto insurance policies and coverage. You first need to know the articles of agreement within each auto insurance policy, including its costs and its limitations. Having this knowledge will help determine your best option, not only for your own insurance, but also in what coverages apply to you and your accident.

This chapter explores the different types of auto insurance policies. It gives you a sense of how these all work, and describes the limits of each policy. The chapter also cites examples of settlement cases to further aid your understanding. Auto insurance has three major types of policies: Personal Insurance Protection, Bodily Injury and Uninsured or Underinsured.

Reading this book will not turn you into a lawyer. Rather, it will provide you with fundamental knowledge and guidance on how to handle yourself after an accident. To begin with, let's look at the three considerations when choosing auto insurance policies.

What to Look For in Auto Insurance Coverage

As you go around looking for the most appropriate auto insurance policy, you need to consider the following:

Cost of the Policy

You should first find out the amount of money required for the policy you want to apply for, and also understand what the deductible is. You will want to compare same policies from multiple carriers to figure out what the cost and coverage is..

The Payment Limits

For every policy there is a limit on the total payments defined in the agreement. You should look for a policy with the highest limits of compensation so that you don't have to pay any bills out of your own pockets once you're insured. The limits will vary from company to company. Different states may also have different statutory provisions, which may affect the limits of different policies.

Duration Before Payment

How long does a particular company take to settle the policy? This question needs to be addressed as you try to narrow down your insurance policy choices. Even though duration is highly dependent on factors and events after the accident, the track record of some previous cases may give you a hint of how long certain policies take to settle.

Different Types of Auto Insurance Coverages

Auto insurance is designed to help you after an accident. The most pronounced outcomes of a car accident are injuries and damage to property. When these happen, your insurance company will step in to pay or compensate for the costs. Every policy has its pre-defined ways of doing so. Read on to discover what the three main auto insurance policies are and how they work.

Personal Injury Protection (PIP): Requirement for All Drivers in Florida

Personal injury protection (PIP) is also referred to as no-fault insurance. In Florida, this is a requirement for all drivers. In some other states, PIP is an available insurance policy, but it's optional. Regardless of who is in the wrong, no-fault insurance covers your medical expenses resulting from an accident.

You don't have to be in your car to be covered. PIP covers medical expenses when you are involved in an accident while riding a bike or walking. It also covers you for any accidents which occur when you are a passenger in someone else's car.

PIP, then, is a unique product that covers your medical bills, even if you were at-fault. However, just like any other policy, it has its limits depending on the policy details and state laws.

What Does PIP Cover?

Formulation of insurance policies is based on a forecast of possible outcomes in the event of an accident. PIP was designed to cover the most likely aftermath of road traffic accidents. In Florida, it's a mandatory policy. Here are the expenses that are covered by PIP insurance.

Medical Bills

This is the primary purpose of this package. It will take care of your surgical, optometric, dental and medical treatment as a result of the accident.

Lost Wages

In the event that an accident renders you unable to work, PIP can cover the wages lost due to incapacitation caused by the accident. It steps in to help you recover lost wages.

Substitute Services (in Select Cases)

This applies if the accident results in injuries that will hinder you from going about your household duties. For example, if you are unable to clean due to accident-related injuries, PIP may pay for a cleaning company for you.

Funeral Expenses (in Select Cases)

In some cases, this kind of policy will assist in paying for funeral expenses for deaths resulting from accident-related injuries.

What Doesn't PIP Cover?

It is important to understand the limits of your insurance cover. This will help you avoid over-expectation or any conflict with your insurance provider. To be clear, PIP will only settle bills for personal injuries that are directly related to the accident.

Below are some of the expenses that PIP insurance would **not** cover after the accident.

Damage to Your Vehicle

PIP would not pay for any damages to your car caused by the collision. This can only be settled if you included such an option in your agreement article.

Vehicle Theft

This is not covered by PIP. Instead, stolen vehicles can be paid for if you took a comprehensive insurance cover.

Damage Caused to Other People's Vehicles or Property

If you rammed into someone's car, house or a fence, and ended up being injured and also damaging another person's property, PIP will only be limited to paying your medical bills. It will not be responsible for any other damages resulting from the accident.

Wages and Medical Bills Far Beyond Your Coverage Limits

PIP will only compensate you for up to the limit of your insurance coverage. Any bills that exceed what you signed up for may require that you sue the other driver, if they were at all responsible for your injuries or for the injuries of any other person in your car.

How to Determine Your PIP Limits

Before you choose the limits of your PIP coverage, you need to determine whether you have any other form of health insurance cover. If you have another health insurance cover, you will only have to take the smallest package provided by PIP since the other insurance cover will help in covering other bills. Florida requires a minimum of $10,000 in PIP insurance.

However, in the event where you and your family don't have any other health insurance coverage, you may consider increasing you PIP limit. You need to consider all the possible health and economic effects of an accident. Have this in mind when you determine the limits of your coverage. Options like substitute services and lost wages are worth your consideration.

Note that you can revise the limits of your policy at any time with the guidance of your insurance agent.

Introduction to Bodily Injury:
Its Position in the Insurance Arena

While PIP takes care of your medical bills after an accident, Bodily Injury covers the medical expenses of another person injured in the accident. It also pays for their lost wages if they are unable to work as a result of the accident. This is a statutory requirement in most states.

What Does Bodily Injury Cover?

When you are at-fault in an accident that causes injury to other people, Bodily Injury will do the following.

Cover the Victim's Medical Expenses

It will cover the victim's emergency medical services, nursing and subsequent hospital visits. It will also pay for any medical needs including crutches or wheelchairs.

Cover Lost Wages

If the victim loses wages as a result of the injuries sustained from the accident, Bodily Injury will compensate them. The limits of the compensation may vary from state to state.

Who is Covered by Bodily Injury Liability Insurance?

Bodily Injury will pay for medical expenses and lost wages of the injured party. This person could be: a passenger or driver in the other car, an unrelated passenger in your car, or a pedestrian.

Note that Bodily Injury doesn't pay for you or your family's medical bills or wage loss. It will, however, pay for your legal fees if you are taken to court.

What Are the Limits for Bodily Injury Liability Insurance?

Conventionally, the State sets the minimum requirement for liability coverage. You should consult your insurance provider for guidance on this matter. However, it's advisable to buy more than the minimum state requirement.

This is because if the medical expenses of the injured person exceed your Bodily Injury Liability limit, you will be forced to dig into your savings to cater for any other expenses over the amount covered by the insurance. This is a very important consideration when determining the limits of your coverage.

Bodily Injury Liability Maximum Limits

Bodily Injury Liability Insurance has a maximum limit. The insurance policy determines a maximum amount to be paid for the covered claim.

There are two types of Bodily Injury Liability limits.

Per-Person Limit

This refers to the limit set for each injured person in an accident. For example, if the policy states that the per-person limit is $40,000, this implies that the insurance will pay for a maximum of $40,000 in medical costs for each person injured in the accident.

Per-Accident Limit

In this type of limit, the policy determines the maximum pay-out for every casualty of the accident. For example, if the limit is $200,000, this means that if four people were injured in an accident, then the insurance will pay up to $200,000 for all four people. It will still observe the per-person limits.

In some states, you can combine the property damage and Bodily Injury limits.

Uninsured Motorist (UM) Coverage

This type of insurance works almost like Bodily Injury coverage. The policyholder is covered against any injury and damages resulting from an accident caused by a negligent driver whose vehicle is not insured. In Florida, this is not a requirement. However, we can't recommend this coverage enough. We often tell our clients that this is the most important coverage you can have. This is because there are many drivers in Florida that are either underinsured (meaning their policies don't pay enough to cover your damages) or who don't have insurance at all.

Uninsured Motorist insurance has four variations.

Uninsured Motorist Bodily Injury (UM or UMBI)

This policy compensates you if the at-fault driver's car has no liability insurance cover at all.

Uninsured Motorist Property Damage (UMPD)

This cover is designed to pay for damages to your vehicle if hit by an uninsured driver. It can be used to compensate for hit-and-run cases in some states.

8

Underinsured Motorist Bodily Injury (UIM or UIMBI)

From the name alone you can quite probably work out what this policy's all about. Unlike in UM or UMBI where the liable party is un-insured, UIMBI covers drivers whose insurance liability is not enough to pay for all your bills.

Underinsured Motorist Property Damage (UIMPD)

This policy is used to cover damages if your car was hit by an under-insured driver. This means that the liability is not enough to take care of all the damages caused on your car.

These four policies will cover injuries to you, any other passengers, and any damaged property if the accident was caused by a negligent driver who doesn't have any liability insurance, or whose cover is not sufficient to pay your medical bills or compensate damaged property. It also covers you if the driver's insurance company is not able, or refuses to, compensate you.

Why Do You Need Uninsured Motorist Coverage?

Many states require this type of insurance, although Florida doesn't at present. Below are the main factors that you should consider before you opt for any one of these policies.

Is Uninsured Motorist Coverage a Requirement in Your State?

This is the first card on the table. While Uninsured Motorist Insurance coverage is a requirement in some states, it's not mandatory in others. You should therefore ascertain whether it's a requirement in your state. If it isn't, then you have other cards to flip.

What's the Rate of Uninsured Drivers in Your State?

Florida is known to have the highest rate of uninsured drivers. It's estimated that 26% of drivers are uninsured. Nationally, one out of every eight drivers is uninsured... That should scare you a little bit. Don't just get scared, however, use these statistics to make a decision that benefits you. Remember, many drivers are also underinsured as well.

What About Hit and Run Accidents?

It's common for negligent drivers to speed off after an accident. When this happens, you are left at the scene either injured or with a damaged car, or both. This is where the underinsured or uninsured policy can be used to compensate you for the medical bills or damaged property.

In a hit and run accident, Uninsured Motorist Bodily Injury coverage will pay for medical bills while the Uninsured Motorist Property Damage compensates for repairs if your car was damaged in the hit and run accident.

However, there are different applications to UMDP depending on the laws of the state you are in. Some states don't have UMDP at all.

CHAPTER III

What to Do in an Accident

Accidents create confusing and chaotic scenes. Knowing what do to at the scene of the accident can help you protect your rights.

Did you know that you can lose all your compensation after an accident because of one simple mistake? Yes, truly you can. Many victims have found themselves making mistakes that have made them fully liable for the accident.

What you do and say after the accident may be used against you, and this will end up reducing the total amount you will be paid.

Below is a comprehensive guide on how to conduct yourself at the scene immediately after the accident. Many people have lost substantial amounts of compensation because of this lack of knowledge.

Here is what to do after an accident: stop!

The first thing you should do when you're involved in an accident is stop. However minor the accident may be, you are required to stop. You should endeavor to stop as close to the scene of the accident as possible. Do so without obstructing traffic and turn your emergency lights on. This will alert other approaching road users. Make sure to switch off the engine.

Failure to stop when involved in an accident is an offence. This would make the scene of the accident a crime scene. After stopping, check to see if anyone is injured. If so, call for medical assistance and an ambulance immediately.

Make Calls: Police and an Ambulance

There are several numbers to dial after an accident. The police, an ambulance, and your insurance are the primary numbers to dial. All of them are equally important, and the order of calls is dependent upon the nature of the accident.

Calling the police should be your top priority. On the other hand, if there are injuries that require emergency medical attention you may consider calling an ambulance first. If there are no injuries, just go ahead and call the police right away.

Collect Information

You should collect as many details about the accident scene as possible. Important details to collect include: the names, contact numbers and addresses of any drivers or passengers involved in the accident. Taking details of any witnesses is also important.

Ascertain all that you can about the other driver's insurance details. You also have to establish if the other driver is the car owner. If they're not, go ahead and ask for the details of the owner. Take note of anyone who leaves the scene before the police arrive.

Additional details to look out for include: car registration numbers, vehicle color and model, time of accident, and weather conditions. Do you notice anything unusual about the lights or the road conditions? Take note.

Taking photographs is one of the best options for capturing many details of an accident scene. This is convenient since most modern phones are camera-enabled.

Give Accurate Information

Do not lie, speculate or give any inaccurate information to the police or any investigation officer who will arrive at the scene. Give accurate details to the best of your knowledge. For example, questions about your injuries can be very delicate, since most car crash related pains and injuries may present hours after the accident. If you're asked whether you're injured and you're not sure, clearly state so. Try to make sure that the other people involved in the accident are also giving correct information to the officers.

Accidents Involving Unattended Vehicles or Properties

If you're involved in an accident with an unattended car or property, make sure you leave a conspicuous note containing your name and address so that the absentee owner of the unattended vehicle or property can find you.

You should also report the accident to the police within 24 hours of the accident. If you sustain injuries that prevent you from leaving your details at the scene or reporting to the police, you should do so as soon as you possibly can. Making a reasonable effort to find the owner of the car or property is also very important.

Was Someone Else Injured in the Accident?

If an accident results in injuries to the driver or passenger of the other vehicle, or even a pedestrian, you are required by law to offer reasonable help to those injured in the accident. You may call the ambulance or take the injured person to hospital. You might however need to seek the consent of the person (if they are conscious and able to make a sound decision).

Should I Go to Hospital?

This is a confusing question for many drivers. Should you go to the hospital or wait for the ambulance at the scene? The answer will depend on the intensity of your injuries, and whether or not the rescue team will arrive within a reasonable time. However, if the paramedics arrive at the scene, allow them to assess the level of your injuries and follow their recommendations.

If you believe that you're injured and you're without an ambulance, allow someone to drive you to a hospital as soon as possible. The intensity of car-crash related injuries is difficult to ascertain, and so the sooner you get to the hospital, the better. Make sure the person assisting you reports the case to the police or any other authorities.

Call Your Attorney

This is a conditional move. If you think that you weren't at-fault in the accident, calling your lawyer to investigate is a wise action to take. This is the best way to determine if you can file the other driver for negligence or not. In this case, you'll need an attorney to help you pursue the claims against the involved driver.

Call Your Insurance

This is very important. Whether or not you're planning to make a claim, and regardless of the level of injury or damage, you should call your car insurance whenever you are involved in an accident.

Your insurance company will always take charge of the situation and advise you accordingly on which steps to follow. They will be the ones contacting the other driver's insurance company in case of a claim.

When calling your insurance company, you should provide accurate information about the accident, including the extent of the damage.

Remember, if you take too long before informing your insurance company about the accident, you risk invalidating your claim. This may require you to pay medical bills and/or repair bills from your own pocket. Now that you are reading this, take the time to check your insurance policy to ascertain how long you can take before reporting an accident. This duration varies from one company to another.

When you call your insurance you should provide details for all the other drivers/passengers/pedestrians involved in the accident. You should be able to give their names, addresses, driver's license numbers and vehicle registration numbers. If possible, you could also provide them with the other driver's insurance company contacts.

Other critical details you may provide to your insurance company include sketches or photos, or any witness accounts of the accident, including the witness' name and address.

Ten Mistakes to Avoid at the Accident Scene:
What Not to Do After the Accident

Knowing what to do in an accident is important. Having this knowledge is critical in helping you manage the situation effectively. Nonetheless, knowing what you **shouldn't** do, and learning about the consequences of making certain mistakes, is even more important.

Car accidents are terrible experiences that can happen to anyone. However, doing the wrong thing after an accident can make a bad situation even worse. A single mistake can transform you from the victim to the accused. Some mistakes may interfere with your insurance compensation, and even make you pay for damages from your own pocket.

Let's look at ten crucial steps you **shouldn't** take after an accident.

Leaving the Scene of the Accident

This is a law that cuts across most, if not all, states. If you fail to stop at, or simply leave, the scene of the accident then you are breaking the law. The accident scene is now a crime scene. You may also be charged with a felony, amongst other charges, depending on the laws of the state you're in.

It doesn't matter if you're at-fault or not. Don't leave the scene unless you're injured and need immediate medical attention. Also ensure that you stop at a safe position at the side of the road to avoid obstruction of traffic or any further collisions.

Failing to Call the Police

This is yet another mistake that can incriminate you. Regardless of who is at-fault, or the level of injuries sustained in the accident, don't ignore calling the police. This is important because the police will be instrumental in determining who was at-fault by collecting information from all drivers, passengers and witnesses at the scene.

A police report is one of the most relied upon pieces of evidence that may be used in any court case relating to the accident.

In some cases, drivers may be uncooperative and refuse to exchange information. The police will come in handy here to help facilitate the exchange of information between drivers. They are also instrumental in helping to move the cars off the road and directing the traffic.

Failing to Exchange Information

Acquiring the details of the other driver is important. It's normal to get a little confused after an accident due to the shock. Many people are usually disoriented. Whatever the case, don't miss out on the opportunity to exchange details with the other driver involved.

Failing to exchange information may make your compensation process very complicated. Some drivers may even take advantage of your mistake and manipulate the situation to your disadvantage.

Insurance compensation depends on the accuracy of the information you collect at the scene. Get the name, address, car model, and registration number of the other driver(s) involved in the accident.

Underestimating Injuries

In an emergency, our body reacts by producing adrenaline. This may dampen the sensation of pain until your adrenaline levels go down. In many cases, this has led people to underestimate the extent of their injuries.

In some cases, this may lead to fatalities because serious injuries have been mistaken for minor ones. It's important to always seek medical attention and undergo necessary scans to be sure of your safety.

Admitting Liability or Fault

"Anything you say may and shall be used against you in court." We're all too familiar with this phrase, aren't we? Don't admit liability. Often, people admit liability without realizing they're doing so. When you don't know what to answer, it's well within your rights to remain silent.

Admitting liability is not limited to what you say, it's subject to how the defence lawyers will interpret it in court. It's possible that a simple "I am sorry the other driver is injured" can be interpreted as admitting liability.

Failing to Collect Enough Evidence at the Scene

Don't take chances. Try to gather as much information about the accident as possible. One of the most reliable ways of gathering evidence is to use a camera to take photos or video clips.

Failure to collect sufficient evidence may leave a significant gap in information, or create inconsistencies in your account of the accident. If you're taken to court, inconsistencies in the information you provide may result in losing the suit.

Take account of the witnesses, their names and addresses, in addition to the time and dates of their interviews. Taking note of the road condition, the weather, and even the traffic intensity is crucial for your evidence.

Speaking to the Insurance Company of the Other Party

Speaking to the other party's insurance company may be one of the biggest mistakes you can make at the scene of the accident. Insurance companies can often rush to the scene before your lawyer arrives, and they will try to take advantage of your vulnerability at that point. They will try to persuade you to compromise on your compensation. They do this intentionally because they know, from experience, that most people are not fond of calling their lawyers right away. At this point, your vulnerability will leave you prone to mistakes that could be to the advantage of the other party.

It's a bad idea to speak to the other party's insurance company without legal advice. Let your lawyers handle it for you. Inform them that you're unable to comment until you speak to your lawyer first. Often, they will want to negotiate lower compensation with you. Don't do it, especially because the effects and extent of a car-crash related injury may take longer to show. You cannot establish the cost of treatment in an instant.

Don't engage them at all. Any communication should be done through your lawyers.

Not Communicating with Your Insurance Company

While you have no obligation to speak to the other party's insurance company, you are required to speak to your own insurance company and provide accurate information about the accident to the best of your knowledge.

You must communicate with your insurance company as soon as possible, making sure to do so within the time-frame stated in the article of the agreement.

Failing to inform you insurance company on time may result in you losing your compensation.

It's still advisable to involve a lawyer in order to help you identify any cracks in your case.

Being Your Own Lawyer

Fight the temptation to navigate through the compensation process without a lawyer. Doing this has seen many people lose millions of dollars in compensation. Your attorney will help you to interpret the legal implications of every move as your chase your claims.

Your communication with your insurance company should be verified by your attorney. This means that you need to hire an attorney as soon as possible. This will ensure that all communication relating to the case will only be channelled through your attorney. This is the best approach in the case of an accident.

Not Being Honest with Your Attorney

Be honest with your attorney. Every incorrect piece of information you provide to your lawyer is one step closer to losing your suit. This will create inconsistency of information that will then make it difficult for your attorney to defend you. Your attorney is the one person that needs nothing but the whole truth from you at all costs.

As you tell your side with honesty, you are also supposed to ask the attorney questions that will assist you in understanding every step of the process. It's yourattorney's responsibility to help you interpret the consequences of each move.

CHAPTER IV

Factors Affecting Bodily Injury Claims

What factors affect the value of your Bodily Injury pay-out? Do you know how much your claim is worth? How do you determine your Bodily Injury claim? These are some of the crucial questions you need to ask yourself whenever you are involved in an accident.

The scary part is that most of the time, those who experience injuries end up being paid far less than the worth of their claim. In worst-case scenarios, some mistakes may result in the insurance company refusing to pay you at all.

This is bound to happen if you don't know the factors surrounding the valuation of your Bodily Injury claims. It's equally important to be aware of factors that can reduce the worth of your claim.

Knowing the process of calculating, claiming and contesting counterclaims is important whenever you are involved in such a case. Let's discuss these in more detail to see how they affect your compensation process.

Most, if not all of the factors discussed here cut across multiple insurance policies.

How Do I Get Bodily Injury Compensation?

Unlike PIP, where your insurance pays for your bills when you sustain injuries due to another person's negligence, here you have to claim payments from their insurance company. How you get compensated depends on several factors. One of them is how you prove liability of the at-fault driver.

After proving the liability of the at-fault driver, you need to know how to determine the worth of your claim. Relying on an insurance adjuster is a common mistake many people make. You have to keep in mind that an insurance adjuster prioritizes the insurance company, not you. The adjuster makes sure that the insurance company spends the least amount possible when compensating you.

Determining Your Bodily Injury Claims

Here is an overview of how to calculate the worth of your claim. You may find our law firm's services useful to guide you through this process.

Special Damages

This is the first step to establishing the worth of your claim. This is also referred to as *"hard cost"* because there are visible, quantifiable bills that you incur in the course of treating injuries resulting from the accident. This is a simple total of all your receipts and bills. This should include pharmacy expenses.

Include all bills: those you paid for from your own pocket plus those that were paid by a health cover, if you have one. These bills include: medical or chiropractic bills, treatment and therapy bills, out-of-pocket expenses like lawn care, lost income, etc.

Placing value on general damages (like pain and suffering) can be difficult because there is no set rule on how to quantify these. This is the most challenging aspect to value. However, after a full recovery, you can add a percentage of the total "special damages" as your "general damages" if you have an injury. This will represent claims for pain and suffering.

The total of your general damages and special damages will provide you with an estimated figure for your compensation.

Severe Injuries

If you sustained severe injuries in the accident that may threaten to disable you, get an attorney immediately. The pain and suffering compensation is calculated at a higher rate in this case, and you won't be able to calculate the compensation on your own. Please feel free to give our office a call to speak to an attorney. This way, you'll stand a chance of getting a fair compensation rate.

Reasonable and Necessary Medical Costs

This is another aspect to consider as you calculate the total amount to claim from the insurance company. Note that insurance companies only compensate "reasonable and necessary" medical and related bills. The insurance adjuster will contest any bills that seem inflated. In other words, the bills have to be reasonable.

Medical standards guide the adjuster's case. While seeking treatment, be aware of fraudulent doctors who may order questionable procedures, tests or therapies. Such bills may play to your disadvantage, and give insurance companies legal ground to refuse to pay some of your bills.

When the insurance adjuster notices that you have presented a questionable receipt or bill, they may recommend you visit their doctor for another medical examination.

Where the Accident Happened

Where the injury claim trial is located is a variable that plays a big role in determining the total amount you will be compensated. The insurance adjuster uses "venue" as a determinant of your compensation total. This should be yet another incentive to hire an experienced attorney.

An experienced attorney will inform you about which locations pay more than others. In addition, an attorney will have a good idea of the verdict depending upon where your injury claims were handled. Some locations are known for awarding higher compensations than others.

When an insurance adjuster speculates that the location may not play in the favor of the insurance company, they will try to negotiate with you to accept an out-of-court settlement. Of course, this means you get less than what you would have been awarded in the suit.

However, the location doesn't come with a guarantee. This is just a projection based on the history of similar cases in the same "venue". The best thing to do at this point is to listen to your attorney's counsel. He or she is the only person who represents you and your interests in this case.

Proof of Liability and How it Affects Your Claim

In a Bodily Injury claim, you are seeking to be compensated by the insurance company of the other driver who is assumed to be at-fault. This comes with the daunting task of proving to the at-fault driver's insurance company that **they** are fully liable for the injuries you sustained in the accident.

This is unlike PIP Claims in which you don't have to prove liability in order to get your claims paid.

If you fail to prove liability, the insurance may deny your claims

How to Prove the Liability of the At-Fault Driver

You are obligated to produce sufficient evidence that will lead to a conclusion that:

1. The insured either failed to do something, or did something negligent, that led to the accident and injuries.

2. The insured had a duty of care which, if put in practice, would have prevented the accident from happening.

3. The insured directly caused your injuries through their negligence.

How Shared Liability Can Affect Your Claim

You will get full compensation only if you can prove that the other driver was responsible for the accident that resulted in your injuries. In any Bodily Injury claim, the insurance adjuster does their best to place some liability onto you. This way, they may reduce your compensation amount or even deny your claim altogether. This is part of their job.

Therefore, beware. If the adjuster finds out that there is a shared responsibility, you risk losing the Bodily Injury claims.

Contributory Fault

When the pure contributory negligence rule is applied, insurance companies in some states including DC, North Carolina, Maryland, Alabama, and Virginia can end up denying your compensation. This can happen if they find out that you contributed to the accident in any way, however minor this contribution may have been.

Comparative Fault

Florida is a comparative fault state. This means, if a case goes all the way to trial, the jury would determine what percentage of the auto wreck is your fault, and then the total claim would be reduced by that percentage. For example, if you were 30% at fault for the auto wreck, then your claim would be reduced by that 30%.

In most states, the modified comparative rule is used. In this rule, you cannot be denied compensation unless the insurance company proves that you have equal or more than 50% liability to the accident that caused your injury.

Scenario: How Competitive Fault Can Reduce Your Claims

Imagine stopping at a red light and another driver hits you from behind, causing you an injury. After that, you make a settlement claim of $10,000 to the insurance company of the at-fault company.

Note that, under normal circumstances, the driver who hit you from the rear will be fully liable. However, at the time of this accident, your brake light was not working and so the other driver claims they didn't see you until they were too close.

With this information, the insurance adjuster contested your claims, arguing that you were in fact 20% liable. Under the competitive fault rule, you will be awarded $8000 instead of the $10,000 you had claimed. This is because 20% liability means that the insurance company will reduce the same percentage from your total claims.

The adjuster's argument is not final. You can still challenge the percentage of liability with a counter-offer. This is a negotiable element based on the facts that you have.

At all stages of the negotiation, you are at liberty to consult your attorney.

How Much Can Insurance Pay for a Rear-End Accident?

Like any other accident, there is no fixed amount of compensation for a rear-end accident. The figure will vary depending on several factors including the intensity of injuries and the limitations of the insurance policy.

The major factor that determines your compensation is the severity of your injuries and how the injuries affect your day-to-day life. However, we can provide a rough average, $15,000, for general injuries that do not threaten to render you disabled.

How Long Does it Take to Get a Settlement?

The longer it takes, the more the insurance company will owe you. What does this mean? The insurance company will do its level best to settle with you as soon as they verify facts about your claim. This will help them avoid any extra costs.

However, the severity of your injury and the insurance policy play a key role in influencing the duration within which you are compensated.

In states like Florida, you are likely to be compensated faster if you have serious injuries. Serious injuries tend to put more pressure on insurance companies. It's even faster when the limits are within the policy. It could take just one or two months for you to get a settlement if your claim is within the policy limits.

Besides, it will take longer to get a settlement if you have minor injuries and there are high insurance policy limits. This means that you will have to wait until you are through with your medical treatment.

Compensation for Pedestrians

Let's step out of the car and take a stroll on the pavement. Have you ever stopped and asked yourself: what would happen if I was hit by a car? Would you know how to pursue insurance compensation if you were injured by a driver? Let's answer some questions that will help you understand more about compensation for pedestrians who are injured in an accident.

Who Will Compensate the Medical Bills of a Pedestrian?

Your Personal Injury Protection should take care of the medical costs of an accident, even if you weren't in your car at the time of the accident. Your personal auto insurance should still pay for your bills. If you don't own a vehicle, you can seek compensation from the insurance company of the relative you are living with.

If the relative you live with is not insured, your next option is to use the PIP insurance cover of the driver. Unfortunately, the insurance company of the driver who hit you is not obliged to pay you if you are not a resident of Florida. At this point, it would be your health insurance that pays for your medical bills.

Overall, if the driver was at-fault, then he or she should pay for all your medical bills, either through his or her insurance or pay from his or her pocket. It's advisable to let your attorney lead the way in this matter. Additionally, you can also sue the driver for pain and suffering.

Can I Sue if I was Hit by a Car While On Foot?

This may only be possible if the driver who hit you was at-fault. For example, if you were hit while on the crosswalk, then you may have a claim. In most cases, the insurance company pays for claims without going through the court.

This kind of settlement can be advantageous because it saves you the expenses that come with the court and attorneys. It also saves you the stress associated with the lawsuit procedure. This kind of arrangement should only take place if you are satisfied with the amount offered by the insurance company. If you feel the compensation is unfair, you can contest it in court.

In some states like Florida, if you sustain a permanent injury you can sue for pain and suffering, though this may not apply in all cases. To support your claim, you should use evidence such as photos or videos of any injuries sustained after the accident.

Pain and injury claims can also be made when you have prolonged pain which does not go away. This may need a comprehensive doctor's report. This type of claim may not be easy since the insurance company will consult their own doctor to ascertain your medical condition.

In most cases, the insurance company's doctors will try to challenge your medical verdict. After all, this is what they signed up for. They may argue that back or neck pain doesn't constitute permanent injury. This is when you will require the services of an attorney to help you argue your position.

For Which Injuries Can I Claim Pain and Suffering Compensation?

Injuries resulting from an accident that can qualify for pain and suffering claims vary from state to another. Nonetheless, here are some common pain and suffering claims:

1. Permanent loss of an organ that may lead to an inability to function normally.

2. Sustaining a proven and permanent disability.

3. Significant and permanent disfigurement or scarring.

4. Death.

In Florida, a case involving non-residents may be determined by details of the accident, and not necessarily on the above-mentioned criteria. It's also worth noting that a pedestrian can only get pain and suffering payment if the driver was at-fault. If it's determined that the driver has 0% liability, then the pedestrian will not receive pain and suffering compensation.

CHAPTER V

ᜃᜓᜅ᜔ᜃᜓ

How To Get Your Medical Bills Paid After an Accident

How will my medical bills be paid after the accident? This is a question that resounds in your mind after you've been involved in an accident. This concern only heightens the anxiety and pain surrounding the collision.

The question of who pays your medical bills, and how they do so, depends on the type of accident, your liability, and the terms of the insurance policy that is supposed to settle your claims.

Was it a workplace accident, car accident, or just a case of slipping and falling? These are the questions that need answering before trying to figure how your medical bills will be paid after an accident. In each case, there will be different options for settling your bills and other claims.

Get an Attorney

In most cases, navigating your way through the process of getting your medical bills settled after an accident is quite challenging if you don't **have** an attorney. This is **due** to the **complex** process of claiming settlement from insurance companies.

Insurance companies, via insurance adjusters, will try to part with the least amount of money possible. They do this by attempting to discover loopholes that may find you liable to a certain percentage, or find "fault" in your treatment process that may give them a chance to contest.

An attorney will help you get your medical bills paid by the insurance, and this will help you receive uninterrupted treatment and any medical care necessary.

How Insurance Companies Settle Medical Bills After an Accident

Normally, your health insurance will pay for your medical bills when you are involved in an accident caused by another person, and will thereafter pursue reimbursement from the insurance company of the at-fault driver.

When you get the reimbursement, your insurance company will have the right to ask you to pay them the amount they paid for your treatment. In other words, your insurer will have "subrogation rights" on your recovery. Nonetheless, the insurance company has a limited amount for spending on your medical bills.

For example, if you sustained injuries from an accident (of whatever kind) and the other party was liable, your insurer would settle your medical bills. After that, you would file a lawsuit to claim reimbursement from the insurance company of the at-fault party.

Upon receiving the reimbursement, your insurer would ask that you refund them the costs they paid towards your medical bills. If your insurance company paid medical bills amounting to $5,000, and you are reimbursed $10,000 for medical and other claims (like pain and suffering or any other damages) your insurance company is only entitled to the $5,000 they spent on your treatment, and nothing more.

This is because your lawsuit claimed compensation for more than the medical bills paid for by your insurer. Not everything you claimed and were reimbursed belongs to them (your healthcare insurance company).

However, settlement of medical bills and reimbursements can be handled differently in different types of accidents.

How Are Road Accident Medical Bills Paid?

In some states like Florida, there are specific auto insurance rules for paying

your medical bill, without having the burden of proving the liability of the other party. This is referred to as the no-fault insurance policy. Under this law, a vehicle owner must have a minimum of $10,000 property damage insurance, and at least $10,000 Personal Injury Protection.

PIP will pay 80% of reasonable medical expenses, 60% in lost wages claims, and up to $5,000 in benefits in the case of death resulting from the accident.

However, it will pay for the mentioned claims *after* you pay the deductibles for PIP and property damage liability.

Who is Covered by PIP?

Knowing who is covered in any insurance policy is vital. Under PIP policy, the policyholder is covered, as are any relatives who live with him or her. PIP also covers a person who drives the policyholder's car (with permission) and passengers who do not own a car.

Why Would You Need an Attorney in a PIP Claim?

Often, insurance companies use particular articles in the policy to contest your claims which require you to have a lawyer. Let's look at two common articles that may require you to make that call to your lawyer.

Compensation of "Reasonable" Medical Bills

In this clause, it's common for insurance adjusters to try to neutralize some of the medical expenses as not being "reasonable." By doing so, the insurance company intends to eradicate some of your medical expenses which they're supposed to reimburse you for.

You often need someone well versed in legal reasoning to argue against the controversies arising from these articles. You should engage your lawyer to assist you in solving such a dispute.

The 20% Liability Rule

This rule requires that you pay 20% "out of pocket" in medical bills from the driver's liability insurance cover. It is common for your insurance company to dispute reimbursing your claims under the uninsured or underinsured motorist's coverage. This is another situation that requires you to have a lawyer to help argue your case.

How Are Accidents at the Work-Place Medical Bills Paid?

The fact that you were involved in an accident while at work does not guarantee a smooth compensation process. Normally, the law in Florida requires that a workers' compensation insurance should pay for all your medical bills after an injury at the work-place.

Must I Visit an Authorized Healthcare Provider?

If you are injured in a work-related accident, you will have to visit a healthcare facility or specialist who is authorized by your employer or the insurance company. This is the first and all-important step towards getting your medical bills paid by the workers' compensation insurance. Failure to visit an insurance-authorized specialist may result in disputes.

The authorized healthcare provider will bill your workers' compensation insurance company directly. In some isolated cases, the healthcare provider may want to make you return to work before you have fully recovered. If this happens, you are required to go back to work or your workers' compensations benefits will be terminated.

However, if you feel that you have not fully recovered and are therefore not fit to go back to work, you can challenge this decision. This can only be done if you have sufficient medical evidence and in-depth knowledge of the policy. Since most of us lack this knowledge, don't hesitate to seek the help of a workers' compensation lawyer.

How Are Third-Party Work Accident Medical Bills Paid?

This question is addressed to cases in which you experience an injury at work due to the negligence of someone who is neither your employer nor your colleague. This situation requires that you claim your compensation from a third-party policy. This is beyond the workers' compensation.

An example of this is when you get injured at work as a result of faulty equipment which was outsourced from a different company. In this case, the equipment manufacturer is liable for your injury in this accident, and you therefore have to sue the manufacturer for compensation.

As in other claims, this type of claim will attract subrogation from the workers' compensation insurance because it will have to be paid in your initial medical bills. (Find out more about subrogation in Chapter Ten.)

What Can Make Your Insurance Company Refuse to Pay Your Bills?

For the longest time, insurance companies have been known for being notorious in scrutinizing the details of your claims. They do this with the sole purpose of finding reasons to reduce your payments.

The worst may hit you when an insurance company completely refutes your compensation claims. Let's look at the most common reasons why this may happen to you.

1. When the policyholder made a misrepresentation in the application of the insurance policy.

2. If you fail to cooperate with the insurer in the process of investigating the events after the accident.

3. If you fail to go for treatment within fourteen days after the accident. This has cost many policyholders their compensation.

4. If you don't have a doctor's written report stating that you had an emergency medical condition.

5. If you didn't update information about the number of people residing in your house after purchasing the policy. PIP requires that you keep updating any additional number of people in your household after you purchase a policy.

6. If you presented a medical bill of treatment that is not related to the accident. This can be interpreted as attempted fraud.

7. If it wasn't necessary for you to take any medical treatment. Maybe it was just a small collision that didn't amount to any substantial injury.

8. If the doctor fails to present your medical reports and bills within the time-frame required by the insurance company. To avoid this mistake, it's advisable to go to a doctor who understands how insurance operates.

In all the cases involving the medical provider, the medical provider could sue the PIP, therefore requiring that the jury decide whether the insurance should pay your medical bills.

CHAPTER VI

Increases in Insurance Premiums After an Accident

If you are involved in a car accident, you will often think first about your safety, and second about the damage inflicted to your car. Rarely do drivers think of the effects of an accident on their insurance premiums.

Being involved in an accident in which it's determined that you are at-fault, or an accident which involves high-value property damage, can cause a significant increase in your insurance premiums. Currently, the average increase in insurance premiums after such an accident is estimated at 34%.

The good news is that there are several ways to minimize the increase in your insurance rates. Additionally, some insurance companies offer forgiveness packages to help reduce the impact of an accident on insurance premiums.

How Much Will my Insurance Premium Go Up?

There is no fixed amount or percentage by which your insurance rates will increase after an accident. There are several factors after the accident that play a role in determining the increase in your insurance rates.

Even before other factors are considered, the simple fact that you are involved in an accident activates your insurer. The insurer will look at the accident as a tool for measuring the potential risks you pose for the future. That is when factors like the state laws, your accident history, and age are now put into perspective.

Generally speaking, younger drivers are perceived to be more of a risk to insure than older customers. This means that the rates of younger insurance policyholders may increase by a higher margin compared to older folks.

Every state may have a different increase due to their varying laws and environmental and social factors. All factors considered, some states may have as high as 74% increase in insurance premium rates.

If you have serious and costly damages because of your accident, your insurer tends to increase your insurance rates by a higher margin. This will also be the case if you have a history of being involved in a series of accidents. It makes you look like a vulnerable driver who has the potential of costing the company more money.

How Does Comprehensive Coverage Affect Your Rates?

If your car is damaged by something related to a traffic collision, comprehensive coverage can now be used. This includes situations such as when your car is stolen, vandalized, or in situations where something falls on it, enough to cause reasonable damage. In such cases, you are required to file a comprehensive claim.

Most of the time, this will increase your insurance rates by a small margin, but you must inform your insurer so that your vehicle is repaired.

How Will the State Influence My Insurance Rate?

First of all, you should understand that when an accident happens, it triggers the insurer to start analyzing the probability of the same scenario repeating itself. The higher the probability, the more the increase in rates.

What does the state I live in have to do with this, you might ask. Three major factors enable the state to influence your insurance rate.

State Laws

All insurance policies are guided by the laws of the state. States have variations in limits set to guide the operation of insurers. In some cases, the increase in rate could be influenced by a prior history of such cases within the state. It does not necessarily have to be in the law.

Environmental Factors

Some environmental factors in your state may increase the probability of accidents. The topography is a good example of this. A predominantly hazardous topography will inspire the insurance company to increase their rates, since where you reside exposes you to a higher probability of being involved in an accident.

Social Factors

The general social behaviour and traditions of your neighborhood could also be considered. For example, some states are associated with reckless drivers. This means that there is a higher chance for you to be involved in an accident. Such factors will make the insurer increase your rates.

These three factors are major contributors to the average increase per state. You should try to know the average premium increase rate in your state. This will help you estimate the increase to expect if you're involved in an accident. It's a good starting point on the negotiation table.

Why Do Insurance Premiums Increase After an Accident?

When you sign for a policy, the insurance company gives you the benefit of the doubt and assumes that you are not a negligent driver. However, when you're involved in an accident, the insurer now presumes that your driving style can result in accidents. This means that they have to go back to the drawing board.

Your rates will be revised upwards depending on the nature of the accident, and more significantly, your level of liability. This is not a punishment: it's a calculated probability of you being involved in another accident, and therefore there should be a matching cover for this.

The more liable you are, the higher the increase in your premiums. By having an accident, the insurer feels that you are a riskier customer to cover. Therefore, the insurer simply passes the risk to you by increasing your premiums. However, this increase may be revised downwards after some years, on the condition that you're not involved in an accident within this period.

On the other hand, you can also switch insurance companies if you're uncomfortable with the new rates. No law compels you to stick to the same provider. You may shop around for a cheaper alternative. However, this switch comes with its fair share of challenges. It's recommended that you seek legal advice before doing this. Your lawyer may help you make an informed decision.

What If You're Not At-Fault?

If you are not at-fault during the accident, and the other insurance company paid for all damages, your insurance premium will likely not increase. However, if the at fault party's insurance company did not pay for all of the damages, or if you were found to be at fault you will likely see a policy premium increase. Some insurance companies offer accident forgiveness.

Accident forgiveness waives the surcharges on you as a first time at-fault driver. What does this mean for you? Simple. Your premiums will not be increased as high as they would have been without accident forgiveness. In some cases, the premiums won't be increased at all.

This arrangement is often extended free of charge to long-term customers who have a good record. However, new drivers, or those with not-so-good driving records, may have to pay an additional fee for this program.

When searching for an insurance company, you must do proper research to find out which providers offer this program, and which don't. Even for those who offer accident forgiveness, you have to scrutinise the terms of each company because they come in different packages.

How Long Will an Accident Be on My Records For?

How long an accident remains on your record is determined by several factors. Nonetheless, most accidents may be on your record for a period of between three to five years. This varies from state to state. Apart from the state in which you live, the severity of the accident is another major factor. While minor accidents may take a few years to leave your records, fatal accidents may stay on your records for up to ten years. Visit your state's website to check how it treats each case so that you are not caught by surprise.

How to Lower Insurance Rates After a Car Accident

As the insurance provider seeks to increase your premiums after the accident, it's beneficial to be equipped with knowledge that will help you counter this move. You may not stop the incremental rise on your rate, but you can do your best to get the lowest insurance premium rise possible.

This will be especially helpful if you don't qualify for accident forgiveness from your insurer. In such a case, there are some tricks you can use to control the rise.

Often, you can start by speaking to your insurer about the rise in your insurance rates after an accident. This will help you understand how the increment was determined, and therefore help you figure out how to approach it. The insurer may offer you some discounts depending on your appeal. This is a good starting point.

Let's look at some ways of capping the insurance rate increment after an accident.

1. **Improve Your Credit Score**

   Improving your credibility is a sure way of reducing the rise of your insurance premium after an accident. You should address any credit issues with your insurance provider on time to avoid any discrepancies.

2. **Raise Your Deductible**

Raising your deductible means that you can settle significant expenses before the insurance company steps in. Therefore, increasing your deductible will lower your premium.

3. **Take Advantage of Discounts**

As you sit down with your insurance provider to negotiate the increase in your insurance rate after an accident, make sure you're aware of all the discounts that are offered by your provider so that you can appeal for the applicable ones. If you qualify for some discounts, this will be an advantage. Such discounts may include multiple policies and student discounts.

4. **Reduce Your Insurance Coverage**

Lowering your insurance coverage is another good way of capping any increase in insurance rate after an accident. Doing this will require that you understand the minimum insurance requirement in your state.

From here you can then reduce, or even drop, some of the insurance coverage that is not a requirement in your state. You may also consider signing for the minimum rates for some of the policies that you take. You can reduce your comprehensive coverage, for example. Please note that we don't advise you to lower your insurance coverage.

5. **Go Shopping**

When shopping for insurance companies you may find an alternate carrier with lower rates that are within your budget. For any buyer, this is often a good idea before settling on one product. This is how you get to grips with the details of every policy offered by different insurance companies.

Be aware of elements like discounts, premiums and their increment on rates after an accident.

6. **Drive a Cheaper Vehicle**

As a rule of thumb in the insurance industry, expensive cars are costly to insure. You may therefore consider side-stepping to a cheaper car.

You may also consider not filing a claim for repairs if the cost of repairing the car is below your deductible. This is a smart move.

Claims That Increase Insurance Rates the Most

Bodily Injury is the claim that will increase your insurance premium the most. This is because these claims are costly to the insurance company. One Bodily Injury claim can increase your insurance rates by over 48%. This also depends on the state in which you live .

On the other hand, comprehensive claims are known to have the least incremental rise in insurance rates. These claims are associated with low-cost solutions like minor fixes and repairs. Comprehensive claims can attract as low as a 2% increment in your insurance rates.

The Accident Wasn't Your Fault: Does it Matter?

Unfortunately, it doesn't matter if you were at-fault or not. Every accident will have an increasing impact on your insurance rate unless you are offered an accident forgiveness discount. However, there is a difference in the incremental increase between an at-fault driver and a driver with no liability.

Even in cases where your insurance offers accident forgiveness, it doesn't mean that you will find yourself without a scratch. The accident has already made the insurance company raise their eyebrows. They will now note that you're a potential risk.

When you're not at-fault but you have a history of being involved in accidents, the insurance company still slap you with a premium increase. This is because your previous record is put into consideration.

In other words, every accident has an affect on your rates, or at the very least on your rapport with the insurance company.

And so...

Your insurance premium rates increase depending on the state you live, the type of accident, and the claims associated with it.

The accident forgiveness program is the only way out of an accident without increasing your insurance premium.

Both at-fault and non-fault drivers will have their rates increased. Being at-fault increases your rates by a bigger margin compared with the increase in rates if you were not at-fault.

That said, there are several ways to prevent your premiums from soaring too high after an accident. Opting for a cheaper car, improving your debt score, and adjusting your policy are among the tricks to prevent your insurance rates from getting too high.

Generally speaking, you should not think of the increase in your insurance rates as a punishment from the insurance company. This is based on the risk factors and the increased probability of you getting in another accident.

CHAPTER VII

ﾟ◦✧◦ﾟ

Uber Car Accident Settlements

Accidents involving ride-sharing cars have some unique guidelines to follow to get compensation for your injuries and damages. This is because insurance companies have customized special packages to compensate the victims of Uber accidents. Therefore, you also need to look for an attorney who has a good understanding of Uber accident claims if you are injured in an Uber accident.

This guideline is good for both drivers and passengers involved in Uber accidents. It focuses on how to seek a settlement in the event someone is involved in an accident while driving or boarding an Uber.

What to Do in an Uber Accident

Like all other car accidents, you are required to dial 911 as soon as you can when involved in an accident with Uber. You should also seek treatment immediately. Taking too long to seek medical care after the accident may give the insurance adjuster grounds to reduce your injury claims.

In Florida and select states, it's a requirement that Uber provide PIP insurance to the Uber driver in specific situations. For example, if the driver has his Uber driver app on, but is not picking up a passenger, then in the case of an accident the insurer will pay up to $10,000 in medical bills.

Responding to questions from Uber, the insurance company, or any party other than the police may be disastrous to your case. Always know that you have the right to remain silent, and to speak only in the presence of your lawyer, or after receiving his or her guidance.

If you don't intend to hire an attorney, you should be extremely careful with every statement you make. The insurance company is looking for the slightest weakness in your statement so that they can use this against you. The insurance adjusters will seek out any of your comments that could weaken your case.

Overall, it's highly recommended that you hire an attorney, especially because Uber cases can be challenging.

Should You Engage an Attorney?

You must seek the services of an attorney in the state where the accident happened. This is simply because every state has varying articles about Uber accidents. Many Uber attorneys offer you free consultations and will only charge you if you're compensated. So don't hesitate to call one.

Hiring an attorney relieves you from the stress that comes with an accident. Avoid dealing with insurance companies directly at all costs, unless you're sure that you're well informed on insurance matters. It's very difficult to know when and when not to speak in dealing with other parties in an Uber accident.

However, there's good news: Uber insurance covers a wide range of injury and damage claims. This is a blessing for many uninsured drivers.

The Fate of Uber Passengers

For Uber passengers, the insurer will only pay for the Personal Injury claims after the passenger claims Bodily Injury Liability compensation from the other car's insurance. Only then could you claim UM from Uber's insurance company. This means that Uber passengers' injury claims will only be paid if there was no other driver liable for the injuries resulting from the accident.

Uber's Uninsured Motorist coverage can pay a maximum of $250,000 if the Uber driver is fully liable for the injuries. In all claims, the passenger can get up to $1,000,000 if the driver is found to be liable.

Generally speaking, compared to normal car accident insurance limits, Uber's insurance covers have higher limits. This is good news for the injured passenger.

Uber's insurance company will pay for your claims even if you were in another car that was hit by an Uber driver. However, the insurance company will only pay if the Uber driver was at-fault. In that case, you will be paid for your injuries and any damages on your vehicle as a result of the accident.

Lower Payments in Uber Accident Claims

It's generally the case that if the Uber wasn't on its way to pick up a passenger, the insurance company will offer very low limits for compensation. The Bodily Injury Liability coverage claims are limited to $50,000 per person and have a $100,000 limit per accident.

While these are the rates in Florida, other states may pay just half of this amount. For property damage liability Uber insurance may pay up to $25,000

It's therefore important to note that the rates vary depending on different factors for Uber accidents.

Companies That Insure Uber Accidents

There are many insurance companies across the U.S. However, only a few companies insure Uber car accidents. Up to March 2020 Liberty Mutual, Farmers Insurance, Allstate and Progressive all insure Uber car accidents in the U.S.

Your lawyer will help you understand more about the companies that insure Uber accidents. You should also know the policy limits offered by individual insurance companies concerning the insurance laws of the state in which you live or where the accident occurred.

Whether you've hired an attorney or not, this is crucial information that you should know as you pursue your claims. It will prevent any possible exploitation. In some rare cases, some corrupt attorneys may try to take advantage of your ignorance regarding articles of certain policies and try to exploit you. To avoid this, it's advisable to seek out reputable attorneys.

Fortunately, in Florida the law requires Uber to provide you with such information, including the limits of the policy.

Uber Passengers and Drivers' Rights

Drivers and passengers have different rights when it comes to Uber accidents, injuries, and other accident-associated claims. The passenger always has the upper hand because they are rarely liable for anything. Note that passengers can be liable if it's determined that their safety belt was not on at the time of the accident, and that this act of negligence contributed to their injury.

Nonetheless, if a passenger is badly injured in an accident, they can still be awarded incredible compensation.

The odds may not favor the drivers in the accident, especially if their liability is more than 51%. Apart from Florida and a few other states, a driver may lose all compensation if their liability in the accident is more than 51%.

How Long Does an Uber Settlement Take?

Several factors may lengthen or shorten the time it takes to settle Uber accident claims. However, Uber claims are likely to take much longer if the Uber was on its way to pick up a passenger. This way, the insurance limit is much lower than when the Uber is engaged.

The insurance company will take their sweet time to compensate you, bearing in mind that most Uber car accident claims do not usually involve large amounts.

Stakes will be high if the Uber was waiting for a trip request or the app was on. In this situation the insurance company will be pressured to settle. This scenario presents much lower Bodily Injury Liability limits. In most cases, Uber insurance companies will want to settle cases involving claims that have a value higher than Bodily Insurance Liability.

Passenger's Claims if the Uber Driver or the Other Car Was At-Fault

If the Uber driver is at-fault your claim may be higher. This is because in Uber insurance the passenger's injury claims can go up to $1,000,000 if the Uber driver was at-fault.

If the other car was at fault and it is uninsured, it's unfortunate to say that you may not be compensated at all. The fate of the passenger will now depend on whether the driver of the other car has Bodily Injury Liability insurance cover. Additionally, you will also need to have access to Uninsured Motorist cover of a relative you live with or on your car. Bear in mind that in many states, Uber has minimal Uninsured Motorist cover.

Many people who experience accidents with Uber drivers make the mistake of completing the accident form on the Uber app. This has ended up with many victims' claims rejected because the details they provide on the app are later used against them by the insurance adjusters. A simple, uninformed mistake can weaken your case. Beware.

For example, the Uber driver may have been on the phone, may have changed lanes haphazardly, may have made a sudden stop that caused a rear-end hit, or caused any other blunder that you weren't initially aware of. If you hurry to fill in the form, you may mistakenly provide information that could let the driver off the hook. This would then affect your compensation.

So this is yet another reason to contact an attorney before making any verbal or written statements. As you have probably now gleaned from almost every chapter of this book, there is a distinct possibility that your statements could be taken out of context by defence lawyers, and be used to deny your claims.

Why Must You Repay Your Insurance Company When Uber Compensates You?

The repayment that you make to your health insurance after your Uber insurance settlement is called a lien. When you are compensated by Uber's insurance company for the medical bills that were paid by your health insurance company, you must repay this. Whether they have asked for it or not, you will still eventually have to repay.

If you fail to repay, your health insurance company may sue you. However, some factors determine whether or not you will pay back the lien.

Even more important than the factors that determine repayment is our reminder that you must not heed the advice of whoever's contracted by your health insurance to recover the lien. This party is hired to protect the interests of your insurance company, not your own interests. Allow your lawyer do this for you.

What Determines the Repayment of a Lien?

Among other factors, the state wherein the policy was issued is a game-changer in determining whether or not you will have to repay your health insurance company. Have a sit down with your lawyer so that you can understand the details.

Another factor that could determine whether you repay the lien is whether or not you were fully compensated by the Uber insurance company. If you settled, then you're obliged to repay your health insurance company. If you weren't compensated, for whatever reason, you're not obliged to repay.

In Florida, the costs of an attorney will be reduced from the lien by your health insurance. This is referred to as the common fund. This is mostly the case if your insurance is through the state. Other people who fall under this category are those in county jobs or those employed by small businesses.

Another case where you don't pay the lien is if you're a resident of New York. This is because New York has an anti-subrogation law which may exempt you from repaying your insurance company.

However, this will only come into play if you have a private insurance health cover: one that is not paid by your employer. Your insurance company will not demand repayment from you after the Uber insurance pays you if you were involved in an accident in Florida.

Interpreting these laws, and how they are affected across different counties needs the help of a good lawyer, especially one who understands the differences in Uber insurance laws across different states. Unless you're ready to lose a big chunk of your cash on the negotiation table, don't **be** your attorney, get one.

Uber Accident Pain and Injury Claims That are Worth More Than $50k

Even though many factors are considered in determining the exact amount for compensation, some injuries have been compensated $50,000 and above.

Here's a list of some of the injuries that have consistently been awarded full compensation of over $50,000 in value for pain and suffering:

- Shoulder joint tear (labrum tear)
- Rotator cuff tear
- Tibial plateau fracture
- Broken wrist (distal radius fracture)
- Thumb fracture
- Ankle fracture
- Broken upper leg bone (femur)
- Herniated disc
- Fracture of a bone in your face
- Hip fracture
- Lower leg (tibia) fracture

Even depression and open skull fractures can be valued at over $50,000. In addition to these injuries, spinal fusion surgery can have a value well over $50,000 in pain and suffering compensation.

It's not a must that you undergo surgery on your upper leg bone for Uber insurance to pay you the per-person limit of $50,000 per person. This is also the case in lower leg bone (tibia and fibula) surgery.

For example, a lower leg bone fracture case can be settled for over $60,000 However, if the Uber driver was waiting for a passenger, or was available a $50,000 limit per person may be paid by Uber's insurance based on the assumption that the Uber driver was liable for the injury.

Seven Mistakes That Weaken Your Personal Injury Case Claims

Many Uber accident victims end up losing lots of money in compensation due to mistakes they made *after* the accident and during the proceedings of the claims. When you sustain injuries because of someone else's negligence, you should pursue the matter and make sure that you get maximum compensation for your injuries.

Making mistakes after the accident will neutralize the liability of the negligent party. This means that you'll get less than you deserve. Here are seven common mistakes committed by Uber accident victims that end up compromising their case against Uber's insurance company.

Filling In the Uber Forms After the Accident

Filling in the Uber forms after an accident is a common mistake. The Uber forms are crucial documents whose content can weaken your case. Therefore, it's highly recommended that you restrain from making any statement, written or spoken, to Uber's insurance, especially without guidance from your lawyer.

Negotiating With Insurance Adjusters

Don't negotiate with the adjuster. Just don't! They are not your friends. In this case, they are paid to trick you into signing for much less than you deserve. They thrive by reducing the liability of their insured and saving money for the insurance company. Don't trust the figures they offer you.

Call your lawyers to negotiate on your behalf.

Making Low Demands on Uber's Insurance Company

Lack of knowledge about insurance claims has led to many victims quoting low figures when demanding compensation. Setting a low demand is disastrous because no matter how low your figure is, the adjuster will still try to push you lower than that. Don't stick to the minimum limits. Explore all the options that could help you get the highest payment for your claims.

Dropping the Case Too Soon

When the adjuster denies liability, the case will take more time, and this will come at an extra legal cost. Don't stop at this. Hire a lawyer to sue the insurance company and they will eventually pay your claims. Adjusters will, in most cases, deny liability so that they reduce the expenditures of the insurance company on your case. They are just doing their job. You should do yours too.

Not Searching for All Insurance Coverage Possible

Many victims don't know all the insurance covers that could be involved in their compensation. For example, you might claim for Personal Injury and stop at that, while your case may also allow you to claim UM compensation.

Lack of knowledge in this area has seen many insurance companies failing to pay victims of Uber accidents. But are the insurance companies to blame in this scenario? I doubt it.

Being Your Own Lawyer

This cannot be overemphasized. Get your lawyer at the scene of the accident as soon as possible and let him or her take charge on your behalf. Let it be handled by an expert. This way, you stand a chance of getting a maximum payment.

CHAPTER VIII

Car Crash Accidents

Thirteen Factors Affecting Car Crash Injury Claims in Florida

This chapter focusses on car crashes and the most important factors that affect claims. For any type of accident, there are many factors that determine the success of your claim.

Here are thirteen important factors that determine the fate of your insurance claims when involved in a car accident. They are significant in determining who was at-fault, who will pay your bills, and the value of your claim.

1. **Level of Injury**

    How badly were you injured? The severity of your injury is the most important determinant for the total figure of your claim. Compensation for pain and suffering is based on the type of injuries you sustained in the accident.

    Any injuries that threaten to incapacitate you and make you unable to perform your daily duties (and therefore effect your income) will warrant wage loss claims. In some cases, you will need a competent lawyer to help you defend your claims because most insurers will do their best to undermine this.

    Why? Because this is one of the highest costs an insurance company incurs. Therefore, insurance companies will try their hardest to reduce this compensation. Compensation from wage loss and pain and suffering is the most hotly contested issue between the insurance and the insured.

2. **Was the Driver Under the Influence?**

The driver's state of mind is yet another vital consideration. If the negligent driver was intoxicated by alcohol (or any other drug at the time of the accident) it will attract punitive damages.

In such cases, the insurer tends to offer you more money for compensation because if you sue, they will have to pay much more than if their client (insured driver) was not under influence. Therefore, whether you sue or not, if the at-fault driver was intoxicated, the insurer will have more liability.

3. **Towing the Car from the Scene**

Normally, more money tends to be awarded for pain and injury if the car was towed from the scene of the accident. This is because towing the car creates the impression that the accident was a serious one. With this impression in mind, the jury is more likely to award you more money in medical compensation that if the car wasn't towed.

On the flip side, if you're the one driving and get involved in an accident, don't rush to tow the vehicle from the scene until you have clearance from the authorities and the consent of your insurance company. Taking pictures of the car at the scene is also a very important piece of evidence.

4. **Skid Marks**

For professional traffic accident re-constructionists, skid marks are more than just rubber-bitumen friction marks. They are vital sources of information that can be used to reconstruct the scene and calculate the speed of the car at the time of the accident.

Over the years, skid marks have been used to determine if the driver was speeding or not. It's a helpful component, especially when there are no cameras. It's an effective alternative for proving speed and therefore strengthening the evidence of causation.

5. **How Bad is the Damage to the Car?**

In most cases, a badly damaged car increases the likelihood of a higher payment in compensation. This is because severe damage is associated with the potential for greater injury, as opposed to that of a car which has only minor damages.

If you claim that you were rear-ended at 60 miles per hour and yet your car has no significant damage, it's reasonably difficult to convince the jury that you sustained serious injuries as a result of the same accident. On the other hand, severe damage will easily support the possibility of serious bodily injury.

Additionally, there's also a close relationship between the extent of the damage and the speed of the car at the time of the accident. Some damages cannot be related to a car that was moving at a low speed.

6. **A Written Estimate of the Damage to the Car Involved**

A true estimate of the damages on a car cannot be conclusively drawn from the pictures taken from the accident scene, nor by observation and word of mouth.

This is why it's important to get a professional to assess the damage, and thereafter send a comprehensively written report to the insurance liability adjuster. It will help in clarifying the level of damage which could otherwise not be captured by the photographs.

7. **Red-Light Cameras/Videos**

In Florida and many other cities, red-light cameras are placed at select intersections. They are used to record details like speed, date, time and lane of a car. The main limitation of these cameras is the fact that they only record the car as it enters the intersection, thus capturing the rear view only.

It's difficult therefore to see what the driver was doing at the time of the accident. For example, you cannot tell if the driver was on a call.

8. **The Angle of the Collision: Was it a Rear-End, Side or Head-On Crash?**

A "T-bone" crash and head-on collision tend to be more "exciting" than rear-end accidents. This means that rear-end crashes are more likely to attract lower compensation than side crashes and head-on collisions.

However, don't be fooled. A rear-end accident may still have great compensation if a case is well-built. For example, a recent rear-end accident was awarded a $210,000 settlement. It's important to note that this figure is subject to deduction of the attorney's fee.

9. **Were You Wearing a Seatbelt?**

In Florida, the seatbelt law has different articles depending on the age of the individual involved in the crash and their position in the vehicle. Were you in the front or back seat? The answer to this question has an impact on the value of your compensation.

Nonetheless, it's illegal for anyone to operate a motor vehicle without wearing a seatbelt.

Your settlement would be affected only if your failure to wear a seatbelt contributed to your injuries. In that case, the adjuster would determine the percentage of your liability and then reduce your settlement with the same percentage.

For example, another driver could crash into your car, with you ending up sustaining serious injuries. But if you weren't wearing a seatbelt at the time of the accident, it could be determined that this negligent act contributed 25% to your injury, and therefore your total settlement would be cut by the same 25%. So if you were supposed to be given $40,000, you would receive $30,000 instead.

On the other hand, if it's determined that your failure to wear a seatbelt didn't in any way contribute to your injury, and that the other driver was liable for your injuries, you would receive 100% compensation from the insurance.

10. **Types of Vehicles Involved in the Accident**

The type of vehicle involved in the accident is a factor that influences the settlement. There are two scenarios involved in this. The first is the type of vehicle in which you are a passenger at the time of the accident, and the second is the type of vehicle driven negligently resulting in the accident.

In both scenarios, the Florida laws take consideration over the type of car being driven, and this will have an impact on the final verdict. Being in some types of vehicles may require you to prove that you have sustained permanent injuries that may qualify for pain and suffering claims.

11. **Event Data Recorders**

The event data recorder is a box which records information including the accident history of the car. It can help assess whether the car had been involved in another accident before the current accident, and if so, it will provide the date and time of this prior crash.

Such information is crucial in determining an accident case that involves contested insurance claims. Most modern car models come with this feature. It's like the black box in the aviation industry. However, some old models like the 2009 Lexus IS come with this feature.

Based on such information, the jury reduces or increases your settlement. The figures may swing either way depending on whether the accident history of the car contributed to the injuries or not.

12. **Did the Impact Cause Your Vehicle to Move?**

Based on testimonies and any other reliable evidence, if it's determined that your car was hit and moved a long distance as a result of the impact, your case will be stronger.

Generally speaking, if a car moves a long distance after impact, there's an increased chance that there might be more serious injuries. The testimony of those in the car is vital in this case, and these can be supported by the injuries sustained.

13. **OnStar**

Does your car have OnStar? If it doesn't, I guess you're probably wondering what OnStar is. This is one of the latest technologies that comes with new car models. It's a feature that provides data such as the speed of the car at the time of the accident. It's GPS enabled and therefore also gives the location of the car.

OnStar is an important feature which you should consider procuring.

Information regarding the car's speed at the time of impact is required by the adjusters to assess whether the negligent driver was speeding at the time of the accident.

Knowing the time of the impact is important because this is used to determine if the driver was on the phone during the impact. This is ascertained by checking the call log of the driver and comparing it with the recorded time of impact. In Florida, if the driver was on phone at the time of impact, there would be punitive damages to add to your medical bills, pain and suffering, and lost wages compensation.

OnStar also provides the location of the car at the time of impact. Therefore OnStar is able to answer many questions and queries with regards to the accident.

Most insurance companies ask their insured to have such services installed in their cars. It helps in providing vital information about the accident.

How Airbags and Seatbelts Can Affect Your Case

These two basic safety features installed in every car have their unique way of influencing your case. Deployed or not, the airbag will have a say in the valuation of your claim.

Did You Know that Airbags Can Cause Injuries?

Obviously, airbags are crucial safety features, but they can also *cause* injury. They may cause serious or even fatal injuries because of the speed at which they deploy. If you happen to be too close to the dashboard when an airbag deploys, it's likely to cause injury, especially if you weren't buckled up. If you're injured by the deployment of the airbag and your seatbelt was on, then you can press against the liable parties, including the manufacturers.

However, most cases against the manufacturers are very costly, especially if you didn't suffer incapacitating injuries.

An Airbag Can Cause Throat and Eye Irritation

Aside from the physical injuries sustained from the fast deployment of airbags, you may also experience irritation to your eyes and throat due to the sodium hydroxide in the powdery substance released when some airbags deploy. You are likely to experience temporary irritation. Inform your paramedics if this happens so that this information can be included in your case.

What Happens if Your Seatbelt Wasn't Buckled When the Airbag Deployed?

To begin with, failure to buckle up is interpreted as negligence. This may make you liable for a certain percentage of your injuries, which will reduce your total compensation. Seatbelts are designed to work together with airbags for high efficiency.

So, if it's determined that you didn't have your seatbelt buckled, and that this contributed to your injuries, you will lose part of your compensation.

In conclusion, insurance companies tend to pay more if you sustained injuries when the airbag deployed and you had your safety belt on. Airbags are usually designed by the manufacturer to deploy in moderate to severe impact. Therefore, they are not likely to deploy in accidents with minor impact.

CHAPTER IX

Fraud in the
Insurance Industry

The insurance industry is a multi-billion industry that circulates billions of dollars annually. It's a high stakes business second only to the banking industry. Being a multi-billion industry makes it a prime target for fraudsters. Heavy transactions will often provide fertile ground for fraud.

Who's the Fraudster in the Insurance Industry?

To be precise, every party in the insurance industry has equal chances of committing fraud. The insurance company can steal from the insured, the lawyer can steal from the insured, and the insured can steal from the insurance company. Therefore, anyone along the chain can commit fraud. Healthcare facilities and motor vehicle agents are notorious for colluding with the victim to inflate the medical bills and car repairs or replacement costs.

Initially, all efforts were focused on detecting and preventing fraud against insurance companies, but with time, the target keeps changing.

However, in most of the mega-fraud cases the insurance company is the main victim. Reason? That's where the **big** money is. All parties from doctors, car agents, lawyers and cartels can form a conspiracy to defraud the insurance company. It's always **big** money.

What Is Insurance Fraud?

Fraud is any form of deception against any party involved in the insurance compensation process (with the purpose of gaining financially). This includes faking accidents, providing false evidence, exaggerating bills and providing inaccurate information. When all this is done with the intention of financial gain, it's interpreted as fraud. It goes without saying that fraud is illegal in all 50 states of America. Over the years, the insurance industry has invested a lot of resources towards curbing fraud.

In this chapter, we're going to give you a varied approach to the inconsistencies that may occur in a compensation process that could lead to fraud. We'll examine fraud conducted by the insurance company, legal team and the insured (through false claims or false information about the details of the accident), even going so far as to discuss people who claim a fake death.

In the US, insurance fraud cartels are estimated to fleece more than $50 billion annually. As a recovery strategy, insurance companies will, for the most part, transfer this cost to the insured by simply restructuring their premiums.

Types of Insurance Fraud

For fraud to take place, a lie must be told. False information is the key component of fraud cases. So types of fraud can also be called types of lies. Fraud and lies are inseparable. Let's look at different types of fraud in the insurance industry.

False Claims

This is the most common type of fraud. It involves claims for accidents that never occurred. It can be that these accidents never happened, or someone might have staged the accident with the sole intention of claiming compensation from the insurance company. Some cases can even be stage-managed without the consent or knowledge of the policy holder. Cartels can make claims on the insurance using your name. This is how complicated it can get. Nonetheless, policyholders are involved in most of the fraud conspiracies.

For automobile insurance, many policyholders have been discovered to have lied about accidents that never happened, yet ended up being compensated all the same.

This is usually hard to prove, and so most of these claims are paid for by the insurance company. Arson has also been used in many cases. Property owners can pay someone to set ablaze a building or a car and then claim for more money than the burnt property or vehicle was worth.

Exaggerated Claims

Exaggerating claims is another way scam artists can receive money from insurance companies. This may come in the form of medical bills or property damage. A natural disaster can also provide a conducive environment for such inflated claims to thrive. From car crash accidents to other property damage claims, it's usually difficult for insurance companies to prove the true value of the claims presented by the insured.

Faking Your Own Death

Never underestimate the capabilities of fraudsters. They can go to lengths that you wouldn't possibly imagine. You might have read about people faking their own death in novels, and have probably seen this plot in movies. But don't be surprised to find out that this is a common occurrence in the insurance industry.

With the help of other players who may in some cases be insiders in the insurance company, policyholders can fake their own death. This usually involves a policyholder who has taken a premium life policy. When the death is faked, the beneficiaries receive big pay-outs and then disappear.

Fraud by Insurance Companies and Agents

Pay attention. This is a type of fraud that makes **you** the target. In recent years, there has emerged a new breed of insurance agencies that make policyholders their target. They have several methods of stealing from you. The agencies or agents can divert your premiums or churn your fees. The worst scenario is when an agent or insurance agency pockets all of your premiums.

Many policyholders are falling prey to unlicensed insurance agents who end up pocketing their premiums and who don't pay when you make claims. To prevent this, make sure you are dealing with a reputable agency. Having a good lawyer can also help you identify a reliable insurance agency.

This type of insurance is common with workers' compensation. This is because it involves a lot of money that comes in consistently and it's long term. In another move, the agency will often change the periodical fee for your policy. When this happens, beware: it may be a fee churning scheme that is fleecing you. Especially when the fees keep rising. A good company doesn't change the terms of their policies so frequently.

Auto Insurance Fraud

The auto insurance sector has unique styles of committing fraud. It's an area in the insurance industry where every party stands a chance of losing in equal measures. Unlike other policies, car insurance operates under strict rules that dictate how everyone should behave after an accident. Any inconsistencies can cost the insurance company or the policyholder thousands or even millions of dollars.

To begin with, auto insurance has two broad categories of fraud: hard and soft fraud.

Hard Fraud

This refers to claims that involve stage-managed incidences. The policyholder can fake a car accident by forcing another driver into a collision, or stage manage the theft of their car. Some car owners can plan for their car to be "stolen" to be sold or stripped for spare parts. They could then receive compensation from the insurer. You can serve a jail term for this.

Soft Fraud

These are the most common types of fraud. These are forms of fraud effected by manipulating the facts of a legitimate claim. For example, inflating the bills or value of damaged property, lying about your address so that you can choose an address where the insurance pays more, or simply failing to inform your insurance about some details of the accident and the driver.

When all of these are done with the intention of financial gain, it's interpreted as soft fraud, which is a crime in all states.

Five Types of Auto Insurance Fraud

Many people don't understand the terms of compensation for victims of car accidents. Fraudsters within the insurance industry will take advantage of this to strike. On the other hand, accidents present opportunities for policyholders to lie and commit fraud against insurance companies. Let's look at the common types of fraud in car insurance, especially after an accident.

False Address Registration

Your address is a major factor in auto insurance. People who live in areas that are prone to car theft pay more premium for car theft insurance. Often drivers tend to register details of a different location which pays much lower premium rates for car theft insurance.

Dumping Your Vehicle

This is also referred to as "owner gave up". In this type of the fraud the owner can burn the vehicle, dump it in a lake, or just abandon it somewhere. Simply put, the owner tries to make the car "disappear". They can also sell the car and then report it as missing. This way the owner will seek to be compensated for a stolen vehicle.

Inflated Car Repair Bills After an Accident

This is the game of car repair centers. This can be done with or without the consent and knowledge of the policyholder. The policyholder may in some cases be the one influencing the car repair shop to inflate the cost so that they can share the extra amount. On the other hand, the repair shop can execute this move alone. After all, the car owner is not the one paying. This is particularly common with body repairs.

Replacing Faulty Airbags

Airbags are a very important factor in determining the fate of an accident claim. This mainly affects the medical bills and bodily harm compensation. (See Chapter Eight). Whether the air bag deployed or not can alter the pay-out amount. If a mechanic replaces an air bag that was not deployed in the accident with an already deployed air bag, the insurance will have to pay for this fraudulent act. This type of fraud can earn you up to a year's prison sentence in some states.

Replacing Faulty Windscreens

This type of fraud doesn't require you to be involved in an accident. Some scam artist may approach you and convince you to replace your windscreen with a shabby one that fits perfectly. They will try to convince you that your insurance will pay for this. In reality, they may use your details to claim for windscreen repair from your insurance. This may compromise your insurance claims.

What to Do if You Fall Victim of Fraud

If you suspect that you've been conned by insurance fraudsters, you're supposed to report this to your insurance company as soon as possible. You should also contact the department of insurance in your state and report the incident immediately. This will enable the authorities to initiate an investigation.

How Insurance Adjusters Can Deny Your Case

While we are made to believe that insurance companies exist to help us when the unexpected happens, we may need to rethink this. The truth is, insurance companies are businesses run for profit. If anything, they care more about how much profit they make than how much of a help they can be to you. When the time comes for you to claim a pay-out, they do their best to reduce the pay-out amount to the smallest possible figure.

Since we are talking about fraud, we can take a detour here and discuss some tricks used by insurance adjusters to reduce your pay-out. Is this another form of fraud? Let's just call it a friendly kick.

One thing you should keep in mind is that insurance adjusters are not your friends. They don't work for you – they are against you.

Below are the ten most common tricks used by insurance adjusters to devalue, diminish or deny your case.

Claiming to Be on Your Side

This is a lie. Don't fall for it. An award-winning insurance adjuster is one who makes sure that you get the smallest pay-out possible. He or she is there to find any faults that may make you liable by a larger margin, and therefore reduce your claims substantially. The insurance company is their priority, not you.

By trying to convince you that they're on your side, they're attempting to expose your weaknesses and use these against you in the case.

Discouraging You From Hiring a Lawyer

When the insurance company knows that your case merits a lot of money in compensation, an adjuster will be sent to try and convince you to accept a smaller amount. They will advise you not to get a lawyer, and instead will encourage you to have a sit-down with them and negotiate payment. This way they can take advantage of your legal ignorance and exploit you into paying very little compared with the legitimate amount you were entitled to.

Asking You To Record a Statement

Here is another trick you should look out for. The aim here is to make you say or write something on record that could then be used against you in the case. Insurance adjusters are well versed in taking your statements out of context, and interpreting them to jeopardize your payments.

For example, a word like "sorry" can be used to argue that you admitted liability, while saying "I'm fine" can be taken out of context in a bodily injury case to argue that you admitted to not being injured. This is how cruel the adjuster can be.

Requesting Permission To Access Your Medical Records

The adjuster may ask you to sign for authorization that allows them to access your medical records. That is a handshake gone beyond the elbow. Don't allow it. The adjuster is a master at using these records to discredit your medical claim. In actual fact this is one of the most suicidal moves that you can make. It can destroy all your claims. Don't sign anything without your lawyer's consent.

Asking You To Sign For a Quick Settlement

Don't be in a hurry to sign any settlement before understanding the full extent of your damages and injuries after an accident. Adjusters try to rush you into signing a quick settlement, which, in most cases, is far less than what you were supposed to receive if the damages and injuries were well assessed.

Delaying Your Compensation

Delay tactics are used to suffocate you and make you accept a lower payment. Amid the delay, the adjuster will approach you and ask you to sign for a lesser amount that can be paid faster, rather than waiting for the full amount which will take longer. Resist this and fight on. It's worth the wait.

Snooping Around

The adjuster may in some cases engage a private investigator to record or take photos of you. This surveillance is used to observe your movements in relation to the injury claims you could be asking for from the insurance company. This may work to their advantage, especially if you're faking an injury. However, even if you're not faking an injury, the adjusters can manipulate their material in order to reduce your claims.

Misinterpreting the Insurance Policy

This is a move in which the adjuster downplays the amount you are supposed to receive. They misrepresent the policy to make you sign for less. They mislead you into believing that your case isn't worth much. In some cases, the insurer may even attempt to persuade you that you're not insured. Whatever the case, don't sign any documents to this effect. Instead, call your lawyer immediately.

Denying Liability

Denying liability has been the most common strategy of insurance companies. They will challenge you with unverified evidence to make you feel liable for the accident. The adjuster wants to create an impression that you contributed to a greater extent in the accident, even if this is blatantly untrue. This is an intimidation trick designed to make you sign for whatever they offer. Don't be quick to accept this, let your lawyer take up the case and argue for you.

Challenging Your Injuries and Medical Bills

No adjuster will take your medical bills without a pinch of salt. They will contest the bills and even try to associate your injuries with a pre-existing condition. They're not medical practitioners, so don't allow them to bully you into feeling as though you're on the losing foot here. It's important to call your lawyer because in most cases you might need to go back to the doctor.

CHAPTER X

❧

What Is Subrogation and How Does It Work?

Three months ago, George was involved in a car accident and his car was seriously damaged. Repairing the car would cost him up to $3,500. Since he was insured, he repaired the car and weeks later his insurance company compensated him for the full costs.

It was later established that the other driver was fully liable for the accident and the resulting damages on George's car. At this point, George's insurance company demanded a refund of the $3,500 from the at-fault driver's insurance. George's insurance had to recover the money because it was eventually determined that their client (George) wasn't liable for the accident.

This third-party recovery of cost is what we call subrogation.

Subrogation is a doctrine that protects you and your insurance company from paying for damages that you weren't liable for. It allows your insurer to recover the cost paid by "mistake" towards the damages on your car. Even though subrogation is applicable throughout the entire insurance sector, it's most common in auto insurance.

Everyone has their own way of defining subrogation, and so do we. Based on the example above, we can simply say that subrogation is the process an insurance company uses to recover the cost already spent. The insurance company seeks payment from a liable driver who is insured by another insurance company.

How Subrogation Works

Subrogation happens if you're involved in an accident wherein it's been determined that you're not at-fault, but you've already paid the bills for the accident. In most cases, your insurance may have refunded you all the expenses before this (subrogation) claim happens. Your insurance often steps in to pay for all your bills before the third party carrier compensates. This is because the subrogation process usually takes some time. So, in this case, it's your insurance carrier that deserves most of the recovered money.

At this point, the at-fault driver or his or her insurer is made to compensate. This is often referred to as third party carrier. Your insurance carrier will have to present the at-fault driver's insurance with all the bills to initiate the claim. Your cooperation is required to help in clarifying the details of the claims made by your insurance company.

Subrogation enables your insurance company to recover expenses such as medical payments and car repairs. This also includes your deductible from the liable driver's insurance carrier if you weren't liable for the accident.

Notice that the subrogation process saves you a lot of trouble. Your insurance carrier does all the work, from phone calls to paperwork, throughout the entire process. The process benefits you and your insurance by helping you recover any costs you incurred and yet weren't liable for.

A successful subrogation process should end with a refund of all the costs you and your company paid for.

Subrogation When a Fault is Shared

This is a scenario in which fault isn't clearly defined. For example, if it's determined that you were partially responsible for the accident, some considerations will be made during the subrogation process. This will attract some deductibles. However, this varies from state to state.

Since you share the fault, you can decide to file a claim with your insurance company, then pay your deductible and let your insurer go ahead and subrogate. Your insurance company will subrogate the other party's insurer to recoup all the accident costs. You may receive some of your deductible back. In some cases, you can even recoup all your deductibles. This depends on the laws of your state, among other factors.

Behind the Scenes of the Subrogation Process

When you report the accident to your insurer and inform them that you intend to push for subrogation, they take up the case and everything is done without your active involvement. Remember, all the processes revolve around you, therefore you need to be aware of how you move, behave and what you say about the accident during this time.

Subrogation claims involve some investigation because the third party carrier will not just accept everything your insurance will present. They may need to check and make sure their insured was at-fault before paying. Investigators may be contracted to look for evidence that may be used against you and jeopardize the whole recovery process.

Waiver of Subrogation

Jane was involved in an accident where the other driver was at-fault, and therefore fully responsible for the damages on her car. Jane paid for the repair cost on her own. Now that you understand subrogation, you know that it's time for Jane to report this to her insurance company and to say that she needs subrogation.

However, in this case, the at-fault driver proposes to Jane that they settle the matter without involving the insurance company. Pay attention, this is when a subrogation waiver happens.

If Jane decides to follow the at-fault driver's suggestion of settling the matter without involving her insurance company, then that's what we call a waiver of subrogation.

Note that this keeps Jane's insurance from acting on her behalf to recover the costs. It's best to be knowledgeable about this type of settlement before signing for it. Once you append your signature, your insurance company can't save you if problems arise.

It's important to consult with your insurance company and your lawyer before signing a waiver of subrogation.

Often, the at-fault driver will propose this kind of agreement via their insurance agent. Keep in mind that the agents are skilful and experienced in this trade. They will use all manner of tricks to convince you to sign the papers that will bypass the subrogation process. Your insurance carrier may not advise you to do this. This act puts your insurer at risk of not recouping any funds it may have already paid.

If it emerges that you were paid doubly, a legal matter may arise between you and your insurance. That is another reason you should consult your insurer.

How Long Does Subrogation Take?

While one case may be settled within one month, another may take months to be paid. This simply means that there's no set time-frame for settling a subrogation. It depends on the following factors:

Shared or Unclear Fault

If it cannot be immediately established who was at-fault, then the claims will take longer for a proper investigation to be conducted to determine who was at-fault. The process will take a while until there is a conclusive report from the different agencies and parties involved. This also affects a case of shared responsibility.

Contested Subrogation

When the at-fault driver and their insurer accept responsibility, the process takes a shorter time, unlike a case in which the subrogation is contested. Any resistance from the third party carrier to pay-up means that you may have to involve a lawyer and head to the courts.

Uninsured At-Fault Driver

A case involving uninsured drivers is often a lengthy one. This is because your insurance company has to sue the driver directly. These are not the best cases to deal with. In addition to a driver being negligent enough to cause an accident, having no insurance gives you an idea of the person you're up against. They may not give you an easy ride along the subrogation path.

Who Receives the Subrogation Money?

If you signed a waiver of subrogation, you would have bypassed your insurance company in the process. Therefore you will be the one receiving the money.

However, if you allow your company to take charge of the process, the money will be given to your insurance carrier at the end of the subrogation process. After receiving the money, your insurance company will issue you (the policyholder) with a reimbursement cheque.

What Determines the Total Subrogation Amount?

The total amount you will be reimbursed is subject to the amount claimed from the third party carrier, and the amount recovered. Your deductibles will then be considered before your cheque is drafted.

Calculation of the final amount to be handed over to the policyholder has never been a simple thing. It involves several factors including your cooperation with both your insurance agents and any other parties involved in the process.

The Insurer's Subrogation Rights

This might come as a surprise to you. Just as you have particular rights, so too does the insurer over the money you receive. These rights are mostly put into play when you receive reimbursement for costs by a third party carrier.

If you are doubly-compensated, this should not be the case. Your insurance company deserves most, if not all, of the subrogation money so that it recovers the amount it paid you for the same accident.

Since some people might not want to do the right thing by simply giving their insurer what rightfully belongs to them, there are articles in law that were created to guide the process and also protect insurance companies from such eventualities.

Even though different states have different insurance laws, there are resounding articles that cut across most states concerning the rights of your insurance company to the subrogation amount.

Many books and articles you'll come across will begin and end with the rights of the policyholder. However, understanding the rights of the insurance company is also important. Below are some of the rights of your insurer.

Note: since this book is not intended for law students, below is just a summary of the laws for your greater understanding. It's not a word-for-word extract of the laws of any state.

1. Your insurance carrier is entitled to the proceeds of the settlement resulting from the claim the insured has against any party determined to be liable for the accident. However, the insurer's rights are limited to the amount the insurer paid the policyholder towards the same accident in terms of medical bills, repairs, or any other costs related to the aftermath of the accident. There would be a consideration for any expenses the policyholder incurred.

2. The policyholder can only hold in trust for the good of the insurance company the amount of money the insurance company is entitled to according to the law. Generally speaking, the amount shall not be more than what the insurer paid the policyholder.

3. The insurer is entitled to protection and cooperation from the policyholder so that the policyholder does not behave in a manner that may sabotage the recovery process. In other words, this means that you have the responsibility to do what is right to enable a smooth subrogation process.

4. The insurance company is entitled to receive written answers or statements from the policyholder regarding the details of the expenses incurred after the accident. The policyholder should clearly state their share of the expenses including medical bills, attorney fees, repairs resulting from the accident, and other costs connected to the recovery process.

5. The insurer is entitled to benefits calculated in percentages of the total recovered amount respective to the proportions of each expense including repairs, legal fees and others bills. The insurer is entitled to details of how every figure was arrived at.

6. The insurer is entitled to receive all the documents from the policyholder that are required to facilitate this process, as established by the law of the state.

7. The insurer is entitled to any provisions in motor vehicle liability insurance policies or medical insurance policies that give rights to insurance companies in relation to the subrogation process.

In conclusion, for the most part, insurance companies can place liability on the policyholder. As a policyholder, it's beneficial to understand the responsibilities you owe your insurer in such cases, so as to avoid any crisis or misunderstanding that may cost you.

Benefits of Subrogation

For a process to be legalized and practised by insurers, it must have great benefits to all parties involved. So why subrogation?

1. Subrogation helps the insurance carrier and the policyholder reduce their losses. This is a great way for the underwriters to improve loss ratios. This helps to increase revenue.

2. A well-executed subrogation process improves the relationship between the insurer and the policyholder. It cements client loyalty, especially if it results in a successful recovery.

3. Subrogation improves the security of clients because the insurer is tasked to help the client recover any possible losses. The insurer does all the work as the policyholder sits back and waits for results.

4. Opting to let your insurer lead the way will help you get maximum recovery from the claim as opposed to signing a waiver of subrogation. Remember, insurance companies have subrogation programs with experienced personnel who can help you recover the maximum amount possible.

5. Subrogation saves the policy any extra cost. The insurance company has all the machinery required for the job. A subrogation process needs investigators, legal counsel and other unforeseen expenses. A waiver of subrogation may sound cheap but it may still attract some expenses.

Pros and Cons of Subrogation

Pros

It's a win-win process for both the insurer and the policyholder because subrogation helps both parties recover their costs from the at-fault party or third party carrier.

For the policyholders, subrogation can save you the trouble of lawsuits and possible losses in the event that there was no such arrangement in the insurance industry. This saves time, stress, and costs involved in such proceedings.

Cons

There's double-benefit. If you receive an award from the proceedings of such a process, you'll have to surrender the full amount to the insurer. This includes all the money that was compensated to you concerning the accident.

Did you know that the insurer can sue you if it's determined that you received money from the third party carrier and that you're not willing to submit the proceeds of the recovery? Well, now you know!

Pros and Cons of Surrogation

Pros

Cons

CHAPTER XI

Top Florida
Car Accident FAQ's

I've Been Injured and Believe I Have a Case Against the At-Fault Party: What Steps Should I Take for My Case to Have the Best Possible Outcome?

If you've been injured in a car accident, go and see a doctor immediately and make sure that you receive treatment for your injuries. In the state of Florida, when you purchase auto insurance, the insurance company is required to provide $10,000 in Personal Injury Protection so that you're able to receive treatment for your injuries. You have to seek treatment within the first two weeks, otherwise your claim may be limited to $2,500.

Next, gather all of the records relating to the accident. Some of these records will include:

(1) the Florida information exchange form that was given to you by the officer who responded to the accident **(2)** pictures of damage to vehicles **(3)** insurance documentation **(4)** medical documents from your doctor about your treatment. From here, contact an attorney to discuss your case.

If the Injured Party Was Partially At-Fault for the Crash, Will This Impact the Personal Injury Case in Florida?

Florida is a comparative negligence state. This means that if a case goes all the way to trial, the jury would determine what percentage of the crash is your fault, and then the total claim would be reduced by that percentage. For example, if you were 30% at-fault for the crash then your claim would be reduced by that 30%.

What is the Statute of Limitations or Time Limit for Filing a Personal Injury Claim After a Crash in Florida?

In Florida, the statute of limitations is four years for negligence or Personal Inju ry cases. If there's a claim based on your Uninsured Motorist coverage that's included in your insurance policy, you have an additional year for filing the claim. This means that if the claim is based on the UM coverage included in your policy, you have five years from the date of the accident to file a Personal Injury claim. Regardless of the claim type, anyone who plans to pursue a Personal Injury claim for injuries sustained in a Florida car accident must see a doctor within 14 days of the accident.

How Important Is Seeking Medical Attention Immediately After an Accident?

In the state of Florida, all automobile insurance policies are required to have $10,000 in Personal Injury Protection to cover treatments for injuries sustained in a car accident. Even if the other driver was at-fault, that first $10,000 is paid out by your carrier. In order to potentially receive the full amount of this Personal Injury Protection, you need to see a doctor within 14 days. If you fail to do so, then you would only be eligible to receive up to $2,500 of that $10,000. The statute actually defines the injuries as emergency medical conditions, which are medical conditions with acute symptoms.

How Important Is Seeking Follow-Up Care, Not Missing Appointments, and Following Doctors' Orders?

In every case, the most important goal is to ensure that you recover from your injuries and feel just as well as you did before the accident. It's therefore important to stay on top of your doctor appointments. If you have to reschedule, do so within a reasonable time frame. Missing a doctor's appointment could devalue your claim, since the at-fault party's insurance company could argue that the missed appointment is evidence that your injuries are not as severe as you suggest.

What Should I Do if the Other Party's Insurance Adjuster or Company Contacts Me? Should I Give Them a Statement?

We recommend that you don't provide statements unless your attorney can be present. This is because your words may be skewed in a way that devalues your case or frames it in a negative light. Simply saying "I'm good" to an insurance adjuster who asks how you're doing is something that could be used against you. We only recommend saying, "I've retained an attorney, so please speak to them regarding my care or my condition."

What Defenses Do Insurance Companies Use To Avoid Paying-Out On Serious Auto Injury Claims?

To avoid paying out on serious auto injury claims, insurance companies will tell you (the injured party) that you don't need to hire an attorney. Another tactic is to delay judgement until the statute of limitations runs out, at which point you would be unable to file a lawsuit. In other cases, an insurance company will claim that specific language in the auto insurance policy means that the damages aren't covered. We've also seen insurance companies encourage you to sign a release that bars you from pursuing compensation. Initial settlement offers are always very low, and often aren't sufficient enough to even cover medical expenses.

What Compensation or Damages Could I Seek in a Personal Injury Case in Florida?

There are two types of damages that you could seek in a Personal Injury case in Florida: economic damages and non-economic damages. Economic damages include the cost of your medical care, the cost of traveling to appointments, lost wages, and the cost of any future medical care that you may need due to your injuries.

Non-economic damages include pain and suffering, loss of consortium, emotional distress, inconvenience, and loss of enjoyment of life.

How Is the Value of a Personal Injury Case Determined Under Florida Law?

The value of your Personal Injury case will depend on the circumstances of the case. These can include: medical care expenses, lost wages, how much time you had to take off work, and to what extent you've lost enjoyment of life.

What If I'm Hit By an Uninsured or Underinsured Driver in Florida? Is There a Chance of Recovery?

The most important insurance policy that you can buy is uninsured or underinsured motorist coverage, because it covers you in the event that the other driver is uninsured or has a very low policy limit. This type of coverage is designed to fill in the gap between the amount of compensation to which you're entitled, and the amount provided by the at-fault party's insurance policy (or lack thereof).

What To Tell Potential Clients Who Believe That They Can Handle Their Case Without an Attorney?

The most important reason to hire an attorney is to ensure that you have someone who has experience dealing with Personal Injury claims and insurance adjusters on a daily basis. This will mean that the insurance company will know that they're dealing with another professional rather than a pro se litigant (i.e. someone who is filing without an attorney). In turn, this will signal to the insurance adjuster that you have an experienced attorney on your side who can help determine the true value of your case. Ultimately, having an attorney will reassure you that you'll end up with the best possible settlement.

What Sets You and Your Firm Apart in Handling Serious Personal Injury Cases in Florida?

When you deal with our firm, you deal directly with an attorney. I make sure to introduce myself to every client who walks through the door. By virtue of having prior experience in the hospitality industry, I know how to incorporate hospitality in my legal practice. This means that at DeVries Law Firm, a client isn't treated like a client, but like a family member.

CHAPTER XII

Wrapping It Up

Below is a timeline for your success after an accident. Here is our process for resolving your claim.

1. Confirm insurance coverage for all parties. This is at the top of the list because if the at-fault party was uninsured, you may need to make a claim against your UM/UIM coverage.

2. Continue to receive treatment. Taking care of yourself is the most important aspect of any accident. Unfortunately, getting you back to where you once were can take months to years of treatment and physical therapy. Once your physician says you have hit maximum improvement, we then start the settlement process.

3. Send demand package. Once we hear that your doctor has finalized your treatment, we start working on the initial demand package. This package includes putting all of your medical records together, any doctor's reports on future care, a summary of the accident, and how you're currently feeling.

4. Negotiate with the insurance companies. We then work with the adjuster to try and resolve the case without the need for litigation.

5. File Suit. Should the insurance company not make a reasonable offer to resolve your claims, we then file suit against the insurance company. Even after we file suit we continue to negotiate, but after we file suit, litigation costs start adding up quickly.

Naturally, there are many more steps to car accident cases, and of course there are many particular details that are important to your case. However, these are the initial milestones.

CHAPTER XIII

What Others Say About Our Firm

"The DeVries Law Firm helped me in a Personal Injury case where I was involved in a severe car accident causing substantial injuries. I had to have a lengthy surgery, therapies, and continued to face issues as I will for years to come. Shawn understood the severity of the situation and showed genuine empathy for what I was facing. He was in constant communication with me and made sure I always understood what the next steps were throughout the entire process. I never doubted that Shawn was doing everything in his power to make sure I got the settlement that was warranted. I was very satisfied with the amount in which we settled. I know that if I would have gone to another firm, I would have been just another case and might not have gotten the outcome I deserved. Thank you to Shawn & his team!"
– Leila B.

"The DeVries Law Firm handled my case with professionalism from beginning to end. I was extremely pleased with the results and will not hesitate to use them again in the future if needed."
– Lisa S.

"Shawn did an incredible job. He was responsive answering all our questions, helping us through the process each step of the way. He went out of his way to make sure we understood each detail which could trip somebody up. I was very impressed with his professionalism and attention to detail. I would encourage anyone looking for an attorney who cares to work with Shawn. He will be my first call again if I ever need legal services."
– Jon S.

"I want to thank The DeVries Law Firm for helping me out a great deal. Mr. Devries kept me informed with everything that was going with my case, after a great deal of paperwork Mr Devries file on my behalf and a lot of setbacks Mr. Devries never gave up and I got the answer I wanted. I will advise anyone that is looking for a GREAT lawyer to make sure you call The Devries Law Firm and I promise you will not be disappointed."
– William S.

"Excellent service, punctuality, clear and effective communication. I recommend the service of The Devries Law Firm with no hesitation."
– Jocelyne L.

"He made sure that I was not taken advantage of. I was put at ease immediately after speaking with Shawn. I would recommend him to everyone in similar situation as mine. Shawn provided EVERYTHING over and beyond of what I needed!"
– Laura R.

Made in the USA
Monee, IL
01 July 2025

20365919R00046